The Inside Secrets to Getting Money for Your Non-profit

By Sandra Mizell Chaney

Copyright ©2018 Sandra Mizell Chaney

All rights reserved. No part of this book may be reproduced in any form or by any electronic or mechanical means, including information storage and retrieval systems, without permission in writing from the publisher, except by reviewers, who may quote brief passages in a review.

Cover Design: Present Help Consulting, LLC
Photo Credit: JM Photography & C-Suites Pics®

www.sandrachaney.com

Introduction

Everything we do starts on the inside. What I find interesting is it is often easier to deal with things from an outside perspective rather than within. Look at the cover of this book then look at my picture. By looking at it, are you able to tell that I used to be an emotional wreck; a single-parent, homeless, and someone who attempted suicide? Of course not! Do you know why? Many people only see what is on the outside. Success is often defined based on bottom lines, surpluses and customer responses to a product or service. Like business, what is shown to people doesn't always reflect what is really going on.

Many businesses only show you the good. I did the same thing. I was a "suit." I was a great, successful corporate America suit, who was also fleeing an abusive husband. I had a great job and well, let's just say financially, I was quite awesome as well.

So what does any of this have to do with business – EVERYTHING! Remember I said "everything we do starts on the inside," well this is what was happening on the inside -- the part of me that no one could see. It is also the part of me that wanted more for women and families just like me. On the inside, I needed help. On the outside I looked good!

During my tenure in corporate America, I was a powerhouse, especially in the non-profit world. I used my knowledge, skills and experiences to help non-profits increase funding for women and children. I loved what I did so much that eventually I created and founded my own non-profit. My mission was to help victims of domestic violence. Having had prior success in the nonprofit arena, I was able to secure funding within six months of founding my own nonprofit. I thought this is exactly what I am supposed to do. I took the pain inside of me and used it for good. I was having impact. I was making a difference. It felt right, so I thought.

Since everything was going great on the outside, I really had no reason to deal with my internal struggles. Remember everything you do starts within. What was planted eventually grew and manifested. At this point, I was still masking my life and all its challenges. The more I tried to hide behind the success of my nonprofit and the impact of helping women, the more I became forced to deal with me. All of my work, business and life hinged on me dealing with me.

Throughout this time, I also made many mistakes which cost me in every area of my life, including my nonprofit. I made choices born out of fear. I was afraid of the business running out of money that I made some horrible financial decisions. I brought people onto my board who I thought could help move my nonprofit to another level. However, they were not aligned with what was purposed in my heart to do. I was doing "stuff" and calling it a program. I did not deal with my life challenges and they had a way of showing up and biting me in the butt. So I had some choices to make. I could bury my head in the sand and make excuses or I could learn how to deal with me and fail forward. I chose to rebuild my life and business, but this time it was from the inside.

This was not just about people, but the rebuilding was about me. *Understand this, the sum total of who you are is based on the culmination of every lesson, challenge and life experiences you face.* One thing I did as I worked from the inside, was to surrender and dissolve my nonprofit. I took a sabbatical from what I'd been conditioned and trained to do and focused on me. So, you're asking again

–what does this have to do with business? Well, my answer remains the same…EVERYTHING.

In surrendering my nonprofit, I realized how my impact could be so much greater if I simply showed others how to navigate the nonprofit world. If you are reading this, know that it is okay to start over; to reinvent yourself and your business. There is a tribe of people waiting for you; but if you have some unaddressed internal challenges/things, you will never have the impact upon the very people you are meant to serve. Honestly, this is an INSIDE JOB.

When one hears those words "Inside Job," they immediately think of something horrible such as embezzlement, fraud, theft, etc., however, the inside job is really about you and your business. You have to know why you do what you do beyond and outside your 20/20 peripheral vision. For me, clearing my out my junk including the caked on residue of my pain, eventually led me to understanding why I wanted to help people. It even opened the door to this opportunity. What I know for sure is that I am a heart centered woman. At the core of who I am lives a woman who wants to help others/businesses transcend the norm.

How does this translate into dollars and cents? Well, I have learned that in order to be effective, I must be Inspired. An Inspired leader operates and communicates from the inside out. As a result of my INside and INspired leadership, there is success in every area of my life and in those of my clients. As a result of my transformation, many of my clients have secured millions of dollars in funding.

What I love most is the impact my clients are having in their programs and within their communities. So, here is my question, are you ready to join me on this journey of discovery? Yes, it is about money, but in order to access it, you must go INSIDE.

Are you ready? Good!
                     Let's GO!

Getting Started

You are here because you are ready to start a non-profit or seeking to expand it. Either way, it is good to know exactly what is a non-profit and how to get started.

One key component to having a successful non-profit is to always make sure everything is in order and in compliance. I cannot assume everyone is clear about what it means to be a true non-profit, so let's start with the basics.

A non-profit is a tax-exempt organization that serves the public interest (Not your interest!).

According to the Internal Revenue Service (IRS), the purpose of this type of organization must be charitable, educational, scientific, religious or literary. The IRS has 27 different nonprofit classifications; the most commonly known is the 501(c) 3 classification.

When you receive this type of classification, the IRS has decided based upon your application, you are providing charitable programs and services. It is important to correctly complete the application and NOT assume submission guarantees your organization classification status as a 501(c)3.

Many organizations have applied for that classification, but did not qualify as a public charity and were therefore given the classification of *Private Foundation*. In those instances, organizations had to refile their application because they were unable to receive funding of any kind.

What is the difference? Great question, glad you asked.

A private foundation is a non-profit organization. However, it is an entity that is funded from a single source (i.e., individual, family or corporation) established to aid charitable organizations through grant-making. One of the pitfalls to avoid the incorrect classification starts with completing the application. It is highly recommended you work with a non-profit expert to ensure you are completing the forms correctly. Even if you decide to and want to do it yourself, PLEASE GET HELP! Have someone (accountant, non-profit coach, attorney, even an IRS representative, etc.) who knows what is necessary assist to ensure your application is in order.

The Forms

The IRS uses two forms to determine the classification of an organization: the 1023 and the 1023EZ. Many people struggle to decide which form to use. So here is a simple tip. The 1023EZ is used if your organization is not going to exceed $50,000 in annual funds in the next three years. Additionally, a budget is

NOT required with the 1023EZ form and it is shorter.

To determine if your organization is eligible or meets the requirements for the short form, the IRS provides an eligibility worksheet. If you choose this form, I strongly suggest you create your non-profit's operating budget. Although you do not have to attach or submit it with your application, you will need it for your own use and you never know if and when the IRS may request it.

Remember I said GET some help? Okay, I'm saying it again! There are several organizations you may contact to get the assistance you need. If your budget is small, consider The Foundation Center as a resource and/or the Small Business Administration (SBA) in your state. Each of these organizations has people that can assist you.

If your organization has received its 501(c)3 classification, be sure your organizations 990 forms are up-to-date. They should be filed annually as well as your state business taxes. If you not have filed, there is a good chance your status is in jeopardy.

Why? ~ Let's Start Here

Having a nonprofit is a worthwhile benefit to the community and most certainly the people you serve. Did you know in 2012, nonprofits contributed $878 billion dollars to the economy? Yep, that's right!! --$878 billion dollars is 5.4% of the gross domestic product (GDP).

How do they do that? I can hear all the questions and comments in your head. I was blown away by that number as well. How can your organization contribute to the economy when you are possibly struggling with getting or keeping money flowing into the nonprofit or for the program? Well, read on to discover some simple yet powerful secrets that no one will tell you. The biggest secret to getting money for your nonprofit is simple, knowing your WHY?

What? No? For Real? Stop it! Are you kidding me? It cannot be that simple? Yes, it really is that simple. So let me ask this question, why did you decide to start a non-profit? It is important to know your why for several reasons:

- It will sustain you during moments you want throw in the towel;
- It will help build the non-profit's foundation; and it will
- Help in acquiring funds for your programs.

Knowing your WHY helps make a personal connection that equates to money, which is always the end result. Funders and donors really want to know why your organization exists. Here is another secret: Your WHY doesn't have to be super deep. Just keep it simple but real!

Over the years, I have come across many people who want to create a non-profit or who already have one. The number one reason most heard for creating a non-profit is, *"I want to make a difference in the world."* Even people who work for non-profits express the same feelings.

Desiring to make a difference in the world is certainly a good reason to start a non-profit; however, if you do not understand your WHY beyond the outside peripheries, then it is simply a novel idea.

Let me share some things I believe will help you in understanding your why. How to obtain funding is the number one question I am often asked. Your WHY creates your programs, your personal connections, and your grant score (more on that later). It helps shape how you do everything from recruiting and selecting board members and staff, to; creating viable programs. Even if you have a non-profit and have had it for a while, knowing your why is extremely important. Remember the end result is getting funding to build your programs and services or sustain them. *Your WHY determines a whole lot.*

Here is what I know for sure. There is a community of people you have been called to serve. Churches and government cannot meet the needs of everyone; therefore, you and your nonprofit are needed. Of the thousands of non-profits that are created every year, many do not survive because of mistakes that could have been avoided. Not knowing your Why is one of them!

Consider the following questions:
1. Why are you really starting /have started this non-profit?
2. Is there a need in your community you are trying to solve?
3. Why do you want to make a difference in the world?

Whatever the reason, be very clear; re-read those questions again and again. As you can see, your Why is SO important. What is the end result again – MONEY!

The Why In Your Mission

Starting with your why is key to everything. I have another question for you. What is the mission of your nonprofit? I know I said "***What,***" but there is a reason I am asking. I'm sure you're probably saying "what does my mission have to do with my why – EVERYTHING! Your mission statement seems like something really simple, right? WRONG!

I cannot begin to tell you, the countless number of grant applications I have reviewed where the mission statement is very unclear (even non-profits who have been in existence for a while.) Your mission tells (funders, reviewers, donors etc.) what your organization is all about. The question you should ask is: Are you clear about the need you are trying to meet?

When you really know your why, it drives your mission. Your mission statement steers your organization. For those whose nonprofits have been in around for some time; like nature and people, non-profits evolve. You will need to revisit your mission statement. Does it align with where you are now? Can you see your Why in the mission?

Okay, so let me stop for a minute. I get the feeling you are probably thinking: "I know most of this already." Fair enough! But let me ask another question. Are you struggling to obtain funding? If your answer was "**Yes**", please keep reading. If your answer **No**, then can you stand to be funded at a greater level?

Many people do not think about their mission or their why when applying for funding. It is usually an afterthought or abstract summarization of what you do. Seriously though, your why needs to be in every thought concerning your nonprofit. It is amazing how something that simple can cause organizations not to be funded.

I learned and understood some time ago that money is really currency; and currency flows. Like electricity, there is a current flowing whether the switch is on or off; your **Why** is the current. If it is not properly connected to your mission and vision, your organization has limited to no power.

Why~The Board

One of my strategic alliances once facilitated a workshop and she said three words: Boring, Bored, Board. She was conveying that your Board of Directors is essential to your Why. If your why is unknown you will have a boring, bored Board with no direction.

When starting a nonprofit, most people ask people they know to serve. There aren't any clear directions or strategies in place to effectively govern, so they are satisfying the basic requirement to have a nonprofit organization. The problem is the persons on your board must also connect to your why. It is not just about having a title or even someone who gives a million dollars. If who they are is in direct conflict with your why, they can and will stop or short-circuit your currency (money).

The persons you choose for your Board are major components in your why. Your Board should possess wisdom, have access to resources, and be willing to fundraise, strategically network and be a financial donor. Your Board should reflect who they are at the core. Remember, this book is called Inside Secrets to Getting Money for Your Nonprofit. I hope you are catching my drift.

As you can see, Your Why is vital to the foundation of your nonprofit. Knowing your why keep the current flowing. So before we add some wattage! I'm going to tell you one more thing. People ask me all the time, why are these called secrets. Well, how do you put a giraffe in a refrigerator? You said open the door and put it in right? You didn't say that -- you said cut it up in small pieces. Ha! That's funny. All you have to do is open the door. Seriously, the answers to your nonprofit are right in front of you. They are hidden in plain sight. So...are you ready to discover them? Let's Go!

GET MONEY

Christopher Wallace AKA "The Notorious B.I.G" with his protégé group Junior MAFIA produced a chart topping gold and platinum record call "Get Money" in 1995. What struck me as profound is that Christopher Wallace founded Junior MAFIA, which stands for (Masters at Finding Intelligent Attitudes); and what is even better, he was a social entrepreneur long before the term was coined.

Understand this you are not just a founder of a nonprofit. You too are a social entrepreneur. Google describes a social entrepreneur as:

a person who establishes an enterprise with the aim of solving social problems or effecting social change.

As the founder of a non-profit or social entrepreneur you are building and leaving a legacy as someone who affected the community and changed the world.

Building a successful nonprofit requires you to work from the inside out. Leaders who are inspired understand this and are successful at everything they do. Successful social entrepreneurs are very active in growing and sustaining their field of impact as opposed to focusing solely on their own organization. As a result, money becomes the by-product to help sustain programs and impact a community.

So are you MONEY ready? It doesn't matter how long you have had your non-profit. It's just a simple question. Are you ready? Here we GO!

SECRET#1

Do you know what a rudder is? I had to look it up. I'd heard someone talking about a rudder and steering and had no clue what it meant. So for the sake of being a fifth grader, here is Wikipedia's definition.

A rudder is a primary control surface used to steer a ship, boat, submarine, hovercraft or other conveyance that moves through a fluid medium (generally air or water). You do know that air and water have currents right? Okay, just checking.

You're thinking...WHAAATTT? What does this have to do with getting MONEY? – DIRECTION of course! - Ha! You thought I was going to say EVERYTHING...well, that too but not at this moment. A rudder is like life and business, if you have no direction you are stuck; and what drives your direction YOUR WHY. Knowing your WHY is the FIRST SECRET (we spent a lot on knowing that, so why wouldn't it be your first step). I will repeat...the very first secret to getting money is, knowing your why. I told you everything hinges on that. It drives everything!

SECRET#2 – The Mission

We spent some time talking about knowing your why in mission. Now, we are going to delve a bit deeper into the mission statement. I ask questions for you to really consider and make connections to what it is your organization does. So, does your mission statement clearly align with the purpose of your organization?

When applying for funding, the funder, the donor and even a reviewer must be able to clearly see the connection of your mission statement to your organization. The mission statement is one of the first things asked in a grant application or request for funding. A careful review of a funder will provide you with information of what types of programs and services they will fund. Funders give money according to their mission. Often, they will fund you if your mission is aligned to that of their organization. This is why your mission statement has to be clear. What does your mission statement say?

"The Balance Small Business" page describes a mission statement as "the mission statement articulates a company's purpose. It announces to the world at large why your company exits." There's that why again? You see why your why is important?

Your mission statement should be short and to the point – really no more than 3-5 lines. It should be easy to read and remember. (See Appendix sample)This is not the time to show the world your expansive vocabulary. We know you are smarter than a 5th grader, so keep it simple.

Remember, your mission statement steers your decision making, programs and services. It is the action you are taking; your target audience or the beneficiaries; and the problem or cause you are committed to solving. Consider these questions as you focus on your mission statement.

Here are a few more questions for you to ponder:
- Does your mission statement speak to what you do?
- Does it speak to whom you are serving?
- Does it speak to the problem or cause for which the organization was founded?

EYE SEE MONEY

I like all music genres. One of my favorite songs is "It's a Wonderful World," by Louis Armstrong. The first part of the song, simply says, "I see trees of green, red roses too, I see them bloom for me and you and I think to myself what a wonderful world." This is a vision statement. The song gives a vision of a wonderful world.

Many grant and/or funding applications do not ask for a vision statement, however, a well written one comes across clearly in the application. "The Balance Small Business" page provides a definition of a vision statement as "the destination for the journey of your organization." In other words, it is the dreams you dreamed when you visualized your non-profit. Louis Armstrong's song is the perfect vision statement. *You got to see it before you can see it or you never will see it says Karen Clark Sheard.* Don't forget, your vision must align with the purpose and mission statement of your non-profit.

Here a few things to keep in mind for your vision statement:

- It should be short and to the point.
- Keep it simple.
- It is your dreams and hopes for the future
- It is the mark you want your nonprofit to make in the world
- It is a description of a future you are working towards. (Appendix)

Am I overwhelming you? Close your eyes for a moment. Take a deep breath. Exhale slowly.

Here are a few more questions for you to consider regarding vision:

- What would the world look like if you could solve this problem?
- What does success look like for you?
- What does success look like for those you are called to serve?
- How would the world be different?

There is one thing people rarely think about or even consider when they are creating a business. Yes, a nonprofit is still a business. What is often overlooked is this little word with great impact – **VALUES**. That's right – Values. It is the core of your beliefs. You cannot have a sound mission and exceptional vision if you do not know what you believe.

Go back to what I said in the very beginning; these are **In**side Secrets to Getting Money for Your Non-Profit. An **In**spired leader operates from the **In**side out. If you do not have a clue what you believe, how can you **In**spire, how can you lead? You will not be able to even answer, know or even understand YOUR Why.

The basis of your organization has to be found at core of who you are. What is at the core of your mission and your vision? This is a bonus secret. Every organization should have a value statement that speaks to what it believes.

As a matter of fact, your own life should have a personal value statement. What is a value statement? Glad you asked! A value statement according to the Foundation Center *represents the core beliefs of the organization that inspire and guide its choices in the way it operates and deals with people.* Anyone who reads your mission or vision statement should see your values embedded within. They should also be part of all your communication.

- A value statement should have a minimum of five statements; no more than seven.

- It should guide everything you do personally and professionally.

This is My Value Statement:

I believe love is the foundation to all things internal and that love heals all things. I live a life of freedom, truth and integrity and believe in engaging with the world from a transparent, playful, loving and authentic space.

Everything I do, even in business is driven by this statement. **My core values:** Freedom~Truth~Authenticity~Love~Integrity~Transparency.

What are your core values? How do they guide you and your business? Do they bring out the best in everything you do? Are you still with me? Keep Going!

SECRET #3 – YOUR TARGET

Have you ever wondered why businesses close their doors within the first five years of opening? Ever wondered why so many nonprofits limit the amount of people they can serve? Yes, it has to do with funding; but that's not the real reason. The reason lies in the objectives and the needs the nonprofit says it is going to meet. Did I lose you? Follow me for a minute. A funder always asks what are the objectives and needs of the organization in a request for money. How can you meet a need or provide a service if you don't have a clear understanding of your audience? One of the biggest mistakes nonprofits make is trying to be everything to everyone.

Let me give it to you this way. Remember I talked about my nonprofit. It was designed to help women and families, especially those who were in abusive relationships. As a woman who once was in an abusive marriage, this was my point of pain at one time in my life. So my audience for my nonprofit was targeted to women who were living in my past pain.

Understand this, your target audience is a pain point you once had; and now want to alleviate in the community at large. Basically, your target audience is a reflection of YOU!

That's it! That is secret number 3. Here is another bonus: Funders and grant makers ask about your objectives, needs and the service area. You must answer this question with as much clarity as possible. Points can and will be deducted if you are not clear about your objectives and needs as it relates to your target audience.

Here are a few ways to identify your target audience:

1. **The Problem**: What is it you are trying to solve? What is the need you are trying to fulfill;
2. **Demographics**: Are they men, women, and children? How old? What are the ethnicity/racial profile? What is the educational level? What

is the level of income? Are they homeowners or renters? Married or single? Who will benefit?
3. **Behaviors**: What is their lifestyle? How do they think?? What are they doing?
4. **Evaluate:** Is your program or service right for your target audience? Is it easily accessible?

Funders expect you to evaluate your program. Again, if you cannot articulate who your target audience is compromised or what the need and objectives are in solving the problem, the likelihood of you being funded is nil.

SECRET #4 –Programming, Goals and Objectives

One thing about the secrets I am sharing is they work; and I don't want to keep them to myself. I have a few more, so keep reading.

You ever watch a TV show and begin to like it and then all of a sudden it is no longer being aired. TV executives make determinations about a timeslot for airing a program based on the ratings it receives. Advertisers also give money to networks for specific shows in which their product or service will be advertised; funders are no different.

Funders give money for a product or service that meets a specific demographic and that may have long-term benefits. For many nonprofits, they look for money but often fail short in actually acquiring it. Not because they haven't done the work, but because of their programming.

One of my favorite TV shows is NCIS (the original). It is entering its 16th season this Fall. It has had the same time slot since its premiere episode. The TV executives at CBS make programming decisions for timeslots that benefit the viewer. Like TV executives, nonprofits must be clear about the programs and services offered and the benefits to their target audience.

As a nonprofit, you are responsible for programming. You MUST be clear about your program, goals and activities. Your program paints a clear picture of what you offer. Funders and grant reviewers know nothing about your program, so you need to be very specific regarding the use of the money, if they decide to fund the organization.

Goals

So let's start with goals. What are the goals of the program? Think about the end results of your program. You should have a minimum of three goals and at least one of them should be what you wish to accomplish within the first year.

One key thing to remember is that your goals are not a regurgitation of your mission. They should support and align to your mission and vision. I told you earlier. *You got to see it before you see it or you never will see it.*

Objectives

With your goals, come objectives. These are precise targets that you set a short term. Objectives show what needs to happen in order to achieve your goals. In fact, objectives are simply a road map to achieving your goals. The best way to establish your objectives is to first know your goals.

Now here is where most people get a bit confused. I want you to know this key component in this secret. Your goals are not your activities. Please do not confuse the two. Activities are what you will do to carry out the goals and objectives. In other words, what actions will be performed to get the job done?

Funders really want to know that you can do what you say you are going to do. They also want to know if it is measurable. Don't be that TV show that has much promise but get cancelled because you weren't clear about your goals, objectives and activities and how your target audience benefits. If you don't know what you are trying to accomplish, do not expect the funder to guess.

SECRET #5 Budgeting - It's Not Rocket Science

You are getting closer to the money. However, there are a few other success nuggets you need to know. As a nonprofit, you need to have two separate budgets – operating and program. There is a huge difference in both especially when it comes to funding. I am going to give you some basics differences. Since you will be responsible for your organization, the specifics are solely yours.

Some funders only fund operating cost (capacity builders) because they know you need money to operate. Then there are funders who fund programmatic (specific) things. You MUST know the difference. I cannot stress the importance in knowing the difference. It has, can and will costs you money!

Operating Budget

An operating budget is the organizations expenses, expected costs and estimated income. It includes overhead costs (i.e., rent, utilities, administrative, salaries, supplies, etc.). Those day-to-day things needed to run the organization. Then there is this little thing called the *Indirect Rate*. This helps you determine how much you need to cover the operating expenses for the nonprofit. (This is usually requested in a grant proposal or funding announcement). To get this rate, you simply divide the total indirect cost of the organization by the total direct costs of the organization.

Program Budget

Knowing the goals, objectives and activities of your program has a direct correlation to your program budget. The program budget describes and gives the detailed costs of every program activity that is to be carried out. Your program costs should align with the proposed activities. The program budget should identify which program costs are direct. Understand this: Direct costs are attributed directly to the program; indirect costs happen whether or not the program exists or not.

Listen! I'm sure this is a bit confusing. You should get an accountant that understands non-profit business. That is the biggest take away I offer you. This goes back to one of my very first statements--GET HELP!

SECRET #6 – Tell The Story

Kevin Costner plays a farmer in the movie "Field of Dreams." Throughout the story, he is reminiscing about the greatness of baseball. Several times in the film, you hear the phrase "if you build it he will come."

While watching this movie, I realized that it really wasn't about building a baseball field, but learning the story of his father who had an opportunity to play in the major leagues. All Kevin knew was to build that field, he really didn't know why.

Telling your story goes back to one of the very first things talked about when we began this journey – **Your WHY**. It is important to understand why you started your non-profit. In telling your story, donors, funders and reviewers connect to your nonprofit, especially if you are just starting. Your story provides a human connection to your non-profit. The story you tell gives meaning to the data and facts you provided in your demographics. It adds credence to the program you created.

Here are some additional things you want to be sure to include in your story.

- **Captivate** your donor from the beginning. "Domestic violence is the leading cause of injury to women—more than car accidents and mugging combined", is an example.
- **Do not ramble** in your opening. Establish who you are serving.
- **Describe the point of tension** or the problem. Draw the reader in with your story. This is where your mission and your why is addressed. (your pain point).
- **Be authentic**! Donors, funders and reviewers like authentic stories. It helps them to connect to you and your organization. (No need to embellish)
- **Have a strong conclusion**. Here is where you explain your mission. A potential donor will get a clear understanding of why they should engage with your organization.

The last few sentences, your story should state how your organization works along with how the donor's or funder's support will help the community you are serving. This is your appeal to the donor. Lastly, gather stories from the community you are serving. They are you!

Okay, we're almost done. I'm excited for you already. I know this is life changing. I got goosebumps. Well, here is the last secret.

SECRET #7 –Stay Involved Be Proactive

As I have been writing this book, I wanted to provide you first-hand experience from the many hats I have worn. As a former non-profit founder and executive, I have recalled and remembered the mistakes made and seen. It is my hope that these secrets steer you from making careless mistakes. This last secret is probably the most profound of them all.

I remember hearing Oprah say, "Always sign your own checks." At first I wasn't sure what she meant by that, but then it begin to make sense. One thing for certain and two things for sure, you do not need to be skilled in everything, but you do need to know what is going on in your organization. This is the reason your WHY is so important.

Let me keep this simple for you. STAY INVOLVED and BE PROACTIVE! Ha! That's as simple as I can make it for you. No, seriously. You must remain active with your organization. The Board is there to guide and provide oversight; the staff is there to carry out the goals and vision of the organization. Always keep your WHY before you. It will take you far.

This secret has many ways in which you can remain proactive and involved. One is to build relationships with the community you are serving. You need to know what they need.

The only way to know that is to get out there and ask questions, listen to what they have to say and eventually, they will become volunteers, donors, etc.

The second key is to attend local events in the community you are serving. This is called building relational capital. It is also a good way to bring awareness to your cause and put a face to your organization. One thing funders want to know is how embedded you are in the community. Also, get to know the leaders in the community. They know the pulse of the community. When you connect with them, they will be your biggest supporters.

Third key to this secret is to include stakeholders from your community on your board. Oh yes! You will be surprised at how this helps in shaping your programs. This adds to a diverse and inclusive organization from the Inside.

Keep informed of grant and funding workshops in your area and attend. Many organizations miss out on funding opportunities because they fail to venture outside the walls of their office. I'm telling you, these secrets work if you work them. Research businesses in your area, build relationships with them; you never know if they have a foundation connected to their business and what partnerships and collaborations that may take place.

Finally, consistency, consistency, consistency! Stay Consistent and Involved. YOU are the face of your organization. Roll up your sleeves and get busy. There are people who need what you have and need to hear your voice.

Whew! That's it. You have SEVEN plus secrets you obtain funding (MONEY) for your non-profit money. Are YOU READY to get it? You should be after reading this.

Before we move on, here is an offer I know you can't refuse. Actually, it is another BONUS. For simply getting this book, I am providing you with templates that can help you create a program and tips for obtaining funding and program development plan. How cool is that? All you have to do is visit my website: www.sandrachaney.com

Funding Tips

When looking for a funder or grant maker, you need to compare your organization and its programs to the funder or grant maker priorities. While you are researching, it is a good idea to keep track of your funders.

Please pay special attention to the following:

- Funder's purpose and activities Types of nonprofits or projects the foundation DOES or does NOT fund)
- Application information (including deadlines and preferred method of contacting the funder).

After you have identified some funders that might consider your project, it is important to see if they actually fund organizations or programs such as yours. You need to ask, do they have a history of giving to cause and/or organizations like yours. To find out:

- Check the funder's web site. Most funders have a website that includes application forms, news, reports, and other information
- Read the funder's annual reports, newsletters, and publications
- Contact the funder
- Since funders' interest and priorities change, keep that funder on your radar regularly.
- Create a grant template to use when applying funding.

Commonly Requested Application Questions:

Applicant Information:
- Organization name
- Executive Director
- Website
- Address
- Phone/Email

Project Information
- Project Contact
- Phone/Email
- Length of Requested
- Funds Requested
- Agency Current Budget

PROJECT SUMMARY:

Describe your proposed project's purpose, the service(s) to be provided and the population you will serve, including total number, ethnicity, geographic focus and other relevant details.

Here is a check list of things to include:

Agency Budget	Annual Financial Statement
Board List	990 Tax Form (most recently filed)
Annual Report (If available)	Letters of Agreement from collaborating organizations

Describe the history and expertise of your agency.

Include what your agency does, the composition of your staff and board, and whom you have traditionally served or targeted (geographic area or neighborhood, ethnicity or other factors that identify your service community).

What other agencies or associations do you work with to address the needs of your clients? What is your working relationship with these agencies or associations?

What are the specific community needs or problems that you are trying to solve through the proposed project? Provide agency and/or local statistics or data that help illustrate these concerns, and describe your proposed clients (e.g., gender, age, geography, and ethnicity).

Grant Reviewer Material

Here are some very common mistakes made in funding applications:

- **Not reading the Funding Opportunity Announcement (FOA) or Request for Proposal (RFP):** It is obvious to a reviewer that the grant writer did not thoroughly read the FOA or RFP. Not taking the time to read and understand the requirements, program scope and ask questions can kill a grant proposal.

- **Broad or generic proposals:** Your grant application and goals should complement the goals of the granting agency. This goes back to the first goal – read the funding announcement. What is the grant makers mission or purpose? Does it align with your project goal and purpose?

- **Lacking details:** Certain details of your organization and mission will be so obvious and so familiar to you that you won't even think to include them. However, always remember, people reading your grant may be hearing of your nonprofit for the first time. Even if you know the grantor, or have received funding from them before, you should still provide complete information about your nonprofit. Offer strong details about the actions you will take to address the problem of your target audience.

- **Too much detail:** It is important for your grant proposal to tell a compelling story, however don't get carried away with a lot of unnecessary information. You need to get to the point quickly and use concise, objective examples to illustrate your successes.

- **Be careful not to place** a lot of emphasis on the why while forgetting about the how. Your why and mission is important. However, after stating the problems, your proposal must focus on presenting step-by-step solutions.

- **Terrible writing**: The reviewer reading your grant will probably have read many others that same day. This means reviewers will have little patience for bad writing. Make sure your proposal is reader-friendly, and that it tells a compelling story without being overly sentimental. Write a clear, informative and engaging grant proposal that reviewers will actually enjoy reading.

- **Lack of data:** Granting agencies want to see your statistics. They want to know that your objectives and your results are quantifiable. To show that you are knowledgeable about your area, your grant should include historical data, statistical analysis, graphs and figures, and long-term projections whenever appropriate.

- **Recycled grant templates:** This is major; not that the other mistakes are not. However this could take the grant proposal out of eligibility. It is okay to use a template, however, please update information based on what the funding announcement is requesting. Reviewers can tell if it was recycled.

There are so many more mistakes to list. However, the ones listed are so common, that even non-profits who have been around for years make many of these mistakes. They forget when applying for funding, there is always a different group of people reviewing their grant application. Do not assume anything. Always dot your I's and cross your T's.

My Final Thoughts

You are probably wondering why these things are considered Inside secrets. Well, if every non-profit did just these things, they would be in a better position. A lot of people do not know what it takes to get money for their organization. They have a hit or miss mentality. I should know, not only do I review grants, I also Chair the review panels.

There is so much more I could share with you, but I think this is a great start. If every non-profit did the things suggested in this book, they would not be a secret.

So listen, let me say this and dispel a myth or break a thought. Just because you start a non-profit does not mean POOR or BROKE. I have worked in several non-profit organizations who struggled unnecessarily. When you start with your why and align everything and everyone with that, your non-profit has a better chance of succeeding.

The world is waiting on you. Non-profits are the answer to so many social ills; the government is not. When you forget your WHY, the struggle begins. When you allow outside forces to drive everything you do, expect some struggle. Challenges are one thing, struggle is something entirely different. Remember, inspired leaders understand that they must work from the inside out, not the other way around.

If you are reading this, then of course you are feeling the pull to start your non-profit, revamp it or take it to the next level. Either way, you are needed; and funders and grant makers are looking for some fresh, new and innovative programs. Starting a non-profit, creating your programs, and funding your programs are not as hard as you think. Everything you need starts within.

I told you before, when I created my non-profit all I had was a passion to see women heal from domestic violence. I filed my paperwork, created a board, a budget and my program. After filing my paper work, I started reaching out to funders through letters and proposal writing. Before I received my 501(c) 3 status, I obtained funding from two sources. I cannot say this or stress it enough, **GET CLEAR on your WHY and your Core Values**.

Oh, you are probably wondering how I received funding before I received my status. Well, as long as you have your status by the end of the year, you can start receiving funding from donors. You really want to know how I did it, hit me up (as the young people would say). LOL!

Well, I'll ask again. Are you ready? There's no time like the present. I am here to travel this journey with you. I want help you have impact locally and nationally. It is possible to them who believe. So come on -- grab my hand and let's get busy serving the community and changing lives.

This is an Inside Job!

About The Author

Sandra Chaney, Compelling Change Agent, Nonprofit and Grant Strategist, Bestselling Author, Certified Fatherless Daughter Advocate, National Speaker, Domestic Violence and Sexual Assault Expert.

She is intentional about reorienting and redirecting vested individuals, organizations, initiatives and programs in sustainable ways and with such depth that Sandra is a definitive resource and asset. She has secured over $15 million dollars in in grant funding for non-profit businesses.

Sandra is a recipient of the 2018 Brave, Bold and Beautiful Award and featured in Unbreakable Leaders Magazine, a lifestyle and personal growth publication. She has worked with Clairol cosmetics and Southern Living Magazine to produce a video that trained salon stylists on domestic violence.

Work With Sandra

To book Sandra as a Coach or Speaker or to bring her very successful Inside Secrets to a city or state email us at smchaney@sandrchaneyenterprises.com.

Connect with Sandra:

Facebook: @sandramizellchaney

Instagram: @sandramizellchaney

LinkedIn: @sandramizellchaney

Website: www.sandrachaney.com

APPENDIX

SAMPLE MISSION, VISION AND VALUE STATEMENTS

GOODWILL INDUSTRIES OF AMERICA

Mission: Goodwill Industries International enhances the dignity and quality of life of individuals, families and communities by eliminating barriers to opportunity and helping people in need reach their fullest potential through the power of work.

Vision: Every person has the opportunity to achieve his/her fullest potential and participate in and contribute to all aspects of life.

Values:
- Respect: We treat all people with dignity and respect.
- Stewardship: We honor our heritage by being socially, financially and environmentally responsible.

- Ethics: We strive to meet the highest ethical standards
- Learning: We challenge each other to strive for excellence and to continually learn.
- Innovation: We embrace continuous improvement, bold creativity and change

MONADNOCK COMMUNITY HOSPITAL

Mission: We are committed to providing excellence in community healthcare.
Vision: We will provide an environment of healing that inspires people to achieve a higher level of health and well-being.
Values:
- Care
- Collaboration
- Openness
- Trust
- Excellence
- Performance
- Accountability
- Discipline

www.ingramcontent.com/pod-product-compliance
Lightning Source LLC
Chambersburg PA
CBHW070956240526
45469CB00016B/1428